THE
SPIRIT
OF THE
LION

by

Daniel Meyers

authorHOUSE®

AuthorHouse™
1663 Liberty Drive
Bloomington, IN 47403
www.authorhouse.com
Phone: 1-800-839-8640

First published by AuthorHouse 2/12/2010

ISBN: 978-1-4490-5200-3 (sc)
ISBN: 978-1-4490-5886-9 (hc)

Library of Congress Control Number: 2009912598

Printed in the United States of America
Bloomington, Indiana

This book is printed on acid-free paper.

Contents

THE ORPHAN

On June 6, 1954, in Casper, Wyoming, Margret Eloise Meyers awakened very early, suffering from labor pains. She had trouble standing up straight, but did so as she awakened Edward Peter Meyers, simply called Pete. Pete was a burly twenty-eight-year-old, Stillman working for the Standard Oil Company. Pete, known by some as Oakie, pulled on his dirty Levis and a T-shirt full of holes. After asking Margret if she was all right, he put on his old, worn-out, army-issue black boots, and a faded, green button-up shirt and dragged his tired but strong body to the kitchen and poured a cup of black coffee which reeked with the smell of musky socks. It had been in the old silver pot all night long. Margret and Pete proceeded to get ready to go to the hospital five blocks away. Pete wasn't too excited; after all, this was his fifth child.

There was Mary Kathryn, David Robert, Patricia Susan, Peter John(later called Jack), and Rosalie Marie (later called Rose), who had been born after Daniel Rolph. However, after losing her first son, Margret wanted as many children as she could bear. After several hours in the hospital, Daniel was born at 8:35 AM.

Daniel was born with a full head of hair. Like his older brothers and sisters born before him, he was a towhead. He had all his parts—legs, arms, hands, feet, and so forth—and he was as aggressive as the Wyoming wind when it came to being fed. Both Margret and Pete knew this boy was going to be a challenge. They named him Daniel Rolph Meyers after his uncle, Ralph McGuire. The difference in the spelling of the names Ralph and Rolph is a curious one and remains so, especially since two different versions of why this happened were told. Margret said the nurse at the hospital made a mistake writing it down. Pete said that he and Margret were angry at Ralph, so to get back at him for his lack of responsibility and strong tendency to drink, they spelled Daniel's second name Rolph, with an 'o' instead of an 'a'. Pete and Ralph used to pal around Los Angeles and got into fights. Ralph was a singer, a tenor, and an ex-heavyweight boxer, and he was good at both. Margret and Pete met in Los Angeles after the war. Pete had been a pilot for the Marines, and Margret had served in the U.S.O. Twelve years of marriage, six children, and a long stint of isolation and social ethics in Wyoming proved to be hard on their marriage. Margret and Pete ended their time together with a divorce. Constant fighting had erupted between the two of them over money and Pete's drinking. Margret had difficulty keeping up with the kids and didn't drink; Therefore she found Pete and the kids too much to manage.

By this time Margret had six children—three boys and three girls. Due to the economic situation in the fifties and her being a woman in a man's world, she was unable to feed and clothe her six children by herself. She definitely did not want Pete to get the children and went to court insisting he didn't. Margret won her case. So she put her children into the Wyoming State Children's Home—an orphanage filled with children from similar circumstances.

Five of Margret's children saw this as imprisonment, but Daniel saw it as a new and enlightening experience. His eyes were open and he quickly forgot the tragedies of his past. He completely forgot who his father was and what he looked liked. There was plenty of clean, new clothing, his underwear was bright white, and there was always an abundance of food. He began to receive attention which had been sorely missed at home because of his five other brothers and sisters and two feuding parents. He liked his new home; like Alice in Wonderland, everything was a curiosity—new, fresh, and exciting.

There were games, and puzzles, and other children to play with at the state children's' home. Daniel felt the way some of the other children played was a bit rough, like one boy three times his size hitting him and sitting on him. Daniel didn't know what to do about it. He enjoyed the more structured play that happened in the afternoons on the sun porch, and he especially enjoyed events like Halloween parties and the Fourth of July. Daniel didn't like Christmas much because he once saw Santa in a room drinking and eating without his beard, and it subconsciously reminded him of something hidden in the recesses of his mind about his past. He vaguely remembered a drunken, pushy man who pretended to be a nice Santa but wasn't.

One Fourth of July, Daniel chased butterflies through the green grass and yellow dandelions. The butterflies were yellow with black markings, and as they would land on dandelion heads, he would leap forward with cupped hands to capture them. After great pursuit, he caught one and hurried to show it off. People were milling around everywhere and the adults were admiring his fine catch. One of the older kids asked if he could have the butterfly for his collection, and Daniel, who was five years old, asked, "What's that?"

The older boy said, "I'll show you." He took Daniel to a table where the other kid had pinned many butterflies of all shapes, sizes, and colors. These butterflies didn't move and Daniel was upset. With a pleading voice he asked, "Why don't you set them free?" The older kid replied, "Because they're dead." Daniel didn't know what he meant, but he didn't like it and said, "You're not getting this one," as he ran into the green grass filled with dandelions and turned his captive butterfly loose. He walked around thinking how he would never again catch or keep a butterfly, bee, or any other living thing..

Daniel found favor in the eyes of many of the authorities at the orphanage. There was one particular housemother whom he especially liked. She often singled him out and would keep him with her while the other children went elsewhere. She made up games, and taught him things using stories and rhymes. For instance, when she was tying his shoes, she poetically said, "One over, then under, then make a bow and bow the other. Now fold and pull." He quickly caught on and she was pleased. It was this housemother who sat with him for several days when he had the chicken pox and thought he was going to die. Her constant verbal attention to Daniel gave him the realization that people used language to communicate in order to get what they needed and express their feelings. This revelation of languages' usefulness affected Daniel for the rest of his life, for in it he felt a sense of awesome power.

Although Daniel was a freckle-faced, reddish brown-haired little boy of only five, he liked the ladies. Mrs. Richmond, the orphanage supervisor, who lived in the orphanage, liked Daniel for his intelligence. She often had him come to her quarters to sit and watch television with her and discuss the television programs. The other children in the orphanage were not aware when he shared this pleasure with her. Whenever, Daniel's mother was coming to visit, he would know far in advance of his brothers and sisters. Why he didn't tell them is unknown. Maybe it was so he could feel special during those moments.

Mrs. Richmond seemed to confide in the little boy who stayed up late at night, looking out his second-story window across a field of corn at a baseball park with people cheering. For the longest time he didn't know what the noise was. One afternoon while he was with his favorite housemother, he asked her why the people at the baseball park made noise, and she told him. She also told him not to get caught looking out the window by the night housemothers, or they might move him. He was cautious and was never caught. He wasn't too afraid, however, because he had a friend in Mrs. Richmond.

The most noteworthy incident of Daniel's early years, happened when he was seven years old and had to leave the orphanage for a couple of weeks to go to the hospital for a hernia operation. The other children played too rough for little Daniel, specifically one Indian boy named Cyrus. Cyrus was much larger than Daniel even though they were the same age, and Cyrus liked to throw his weight around when the housemothers were not present. He crushed Daniel in a wrestling match, which resulted in the hernia. One of the housemothers discovered it when Daniel was bathing, and there was a big discussion among the housemothers over it.

Mrs. Richmond was very upset and had a few words with her staff. Daniel was sent to a doctor, —who, it was said, was a horse doctor—and he wanted to operate, so Daniel was sent to the hospital. This was a new experience for him, and he was terrified as the housemother dressed him in his finest clothes to go to the hospital. Upon his arrival there, he was greeted by a slew of nurses and had to go through all sorts of preliminary procedures, like being weighed and having his temperature taken. There was a beautiful nurse assigned to him during the day, and as time passed, Daniel became fond of her. This was his first encounter with strong feelings toward the opposite sex. He would just stare at her when she was in the room, fluffing his pillow and bringing in the water. She continually reassured him that everything would be alright and he should enjoy his stay in the hospital. She liked to joke with him and make him smile. His heart was captured.

There were two other children in Daniel's room, whom he thought were in far worse shape than he was because they couldn't get out of bed. He worried he might end up like them and this frightened him. The day of the operation arrived, and Daniel was given a shot he didn't like much because it made him sick to his stomach. He could hardly hold up his little freckle-faced head. An orderly came and put him on a gurney and started to wheel him down the hall. His nurse stopped them and assured him everything would be alright. Her sweetly voiced words worked their magic and soothed his worries. He had never felt such a loss of control of himself as this. He was taken to a room filled with all kinds of shiny instruments and huge bright lights. There were people wearing white gowns and masks everywhere. An older woman came to him and held a large, black plastic cup in her hands. She told him to breathe slowly and count backwards from a hundred. He began counting: 100, 99, 98, 97... He was out!

When Daniel awoke, there was a woman laying on a gurney next to him. She looked rough. Her hair was displaced all over her head and she was as pale as a bucket of white milk. He was later told that she had just had a baby. When he discovered the bandages around his waist, he thought, "What have they done to me?" and began to worry. Then the orderly came in and wheeled him back to his room. His hospital room-mates looked like they were in better shape than he felt. The next day his mother came to visit him and he insisted on telling her that he wanted to take his nurse home. He was feeling much better. His nurse told him there would be some surprise visitors that day, and there were. At one point, three cowboys covered with dust, walked in, wearing dirty clothes and old, worn-out cowboy hats. They looked like they were straight off the set of Rawhide. The trail boss, the cook, and one of the hands began talking to everybody in the room. They were ragged looking men, and Daniel was filled with enthusiasm when they came to him. They only stayed a short while, but he didn't mind because he was happy. Looking at his mother, he thought his mom seemed so happy with a smile on her face, for the first time in a long time.

The next day, he was put out on the sun porch by himself, where he watched television. It reminded him of the time he spent with Mrs. Richmond in her room. His mom came and the two of them talked about how he was feeling. He asked her when he and the rest of the kids could come home, but she was unable to answer. Then the cowhand from the day before strutted gallantly into the room. Daniel's mom beamed, the cowhand did more talking to her than he did with Daniel, but he did give him an autograph. His mother kept the autograph and it was never seen by Daniel again. On it was inscribed the name *Clint Eastwood*.

Like Moses, who's formative years were not recorded, so it was for Daniel. He finally got to go home with his brothers and sisters, a stepfather and 4 stepsisters. When his spiritual life started he kept a record.

THE SPIRIT OF THE LION

Daniel's first experiences with mental illness tested his stamina and spirit. Some look at the spirit as ominous and eternal, while others see it as a drive or will. There are those who work to control the spirit, both their own and others. They see the breaking and taming of the spirit like the breaking and taming of a lion. Few people live in the spirit of the eternal, for there is no need to do so in today's societies.

Daniel became extremely fearful of classmates, teachers, peers, and family. He had been attending college in Casper, Wyoming, and he was two weeks short of completing his first semester when he began to live a horrendous and enlightening experience. Frightened by what his mind was experiencing, he dropped out of school. He began acting out his paranoia by praying constantly. At one point he held a large, shiny pizza knife with a wooden handle up to his chest in front of Rose, his sister and some friends. Rose asked, "Daniel, what's wrong with you?" Their friends reacted differently. Their reaction was one of concern, but they chose not to intervene. One of them said, "Don't stop him. Let him go ahead and do it!"

Daniel decided not to do what it was he perceived they wanted him to do. He was fearful of them, partly because of their behavior and partly because of the music they listened to—Alice Cooper and the heavy rock and roll of the seventies. He also found their use of drugs and interest in the occult threatening. Night fell and his paranoia increased a hundred fold. His mind began imagining terrors. He felt his sister and friends were part of Satan's entourage, who would soon dispose of him and possibly eat him. He was terrified and found himself lying on the bed face down, imagining them stabbing a knife into his chest to end his life. The group left and then came back and nothing happened. Daniel lay on the couch all night, trying to sleep, but he couldn't. He was cloaked in fear, with his eyes wide open. In the morning, his fears moved him to speak out against his sister, her husband, and a friend. They were shocked and began to discuss amongst themselves what to do. Daniel ran outside as the sun was coming up, he felt this would be the day when Christ would come and rescue him. He also felt immense fear that Satan would use his family and friends to destroy him.

He was fading in and out of insanity, questioning his every thought. His breathing was tense and his heart beat like a cannon ball was being fired against his chest. His skin was cold and his body ached. His sister and her husband came outside, put him in the car, and took him to a hospital. As his brother-in-law held him in his arms while his sister drove, he imagined they were taking him to witness a sacrificial ritual and he would be the sacrifice. At the hospital, Daniel was quickly admitted to second east. At that time second east was the ward for the mentally ill, alcoholics, and the elderly. He was put in one of four solitary confinement rooms which had an extra large steel door locked with a rectangular steel bolt that was four inches wide and twelve inches long. Anyone experiencing insanity—or sanity, for that matter—had to have a sense of what that steel bolt meant.

A female psychiatrist visited Daniel. She frightened him because all the doctors with whom he had previously been acquainted with had been men. For several days and nights, he wrestled with the idea he would be sacrificed. The nights were the worst. He rarely saw anyone, and would stand at a window covered with a metal grate, looking out, thinking to himself, the night would never end, and these were the days of darkness when Satan would rule the world.

The medication Daniel had been given earlier began to take effect. His perspective on religion was changing. His thoughts turned to the words and deeds of Christ, and he began to analyze them, which gave him inner strength. He came to a realization and understanding many times quicker than the rate at which he had deteriorated mentally. He had steadily been deteriorating for about four years during this time, using illegal drugs to keep his emotions more level.

He was not quite sure how long he had been in the hospital, but one particular evening he wanted out. He spoke loudly through a small grated window, in the steel door, about freedom and his rights. He attested to his sanity, saying he could not have clearly or understandably said all he had without some degree of sanity. He voiced the opinion that not even animals were kept like he was being kept. He got an answer soon after.

Six orderlies in white coats and pants barged into the room. As they took hold of his limbs, they twisted them, almost to the breaking point. Daniel felt the pain but ignored it. He had experienced pain in his mind far more deadly and threatening. Four of the orderlies pushed him onto the bed, where the other two forced a straight jacket on him. He could see their faces. The two that were holding him were smiling; the other two had blank looks on their faces, and the two working the straight jacket seemed to be in some kind of mental pain. Daniel suspected that they didn't like what they were doing. He spoke to them and tried to convince them that what they were doing was not necessary. They tied him to the bed and walked out boastfully. Daniel thought their cruelty might have been due in part to his long hair touching the middle of his back. Little did they know he was a young man full of eternal spiritual strength, both mentally and physically. He wrestled against them as if he was wrestling with Satan, and the thought crossed his mind that they, like his sister and brother-in-law, might come and get him for the sacrifice. He managed to get free of the jacket and the bed and was up at the window. He boasted about the power of his God, and preached freedom with tears in his eyes.

The six orderlies came again, and this time, when they broke through the door, there was a fight. One of them backhanded Daniel in the face. They subdued him and the process of stuffing him into the straight jacket began again. This time, however, he chanted the word "peace" over and over again, and all the orderlies assumed serious countenances as they walked out quietly. The light in the room remained on, and Daniel requested that it be turned off. No one paid any attention to him. As he lay tied to the bed, he felt the light and unnatural. Once more he wrestled ... Thoughts ran through his mind like, "How ...g can I continue this battle? There is a whole city of them out there. Surely I will tire before they do." His mind took him to his strength—thoughts of peace and love that he had pondered daily since he was a teenager. This type of thinking was in the forefront of the minds of many of the youth at the time. It was the thinking of the sixties and the seventies. The meaning of life, and the will to endure it and experience it, weighed heavily on his mind. The mind of this eighteen-year-old son of the city was peaking at an incredible rate.

Daniel realized these people were testing his spirit. He would not be broken. He would rather die. He got free from the bonds again, after kneeling and praying. He took his time going to the door. He went to the window again, and shouted as if to prod the jackals who were hounding him. When he got there he started a little slower this time because he was tired. He spoke of freedom and those who had advocated it, such as Abraham Lincoln and Jesus Christ. The sound of many shoes coming down the hall alerted him that the orderlies were returning. He put the bed between himself and the door. They still burst through, and this time all of them held him. He acted submissively and allowed them to twist and jerk him around. To his surprise, a nurse walked in. They pulled down his white pajamas and she gave him a shot in the rump while the orderlies held him firmly. Daniel knew he was in big trouble. This shot would put him to sleep or kill him, and he started reciting the Lord's Prayer out loud as best he could since he did not know all the words. The orderlies continued to hold him and the nurse left. One of the orderlies hit him a couple times and another said, "This is the kind of straight jacket they use in Evanston. He'll never get out of this." That was all that needed be said, Daniel always felt he was akin to the lion, and he reached into his soul for the strength he needed. When they left, he methodically used his strength while still conserving it because he felt it would take him longer to loosen the bonds.

He was free once more and went again to the window, with a calm voice he let those whose ears were out there hear the sound of his freedom. Tired and worn out like a lion after battle, he stepped over to his bed in the small room and began thinking to himself. He pondered the idea that if he fell asleep he might awaken with his father in heaven, or would he remain there in the room? In either case, he felt he was a sure victor.

The three sixes, 666—the orderlies—did not defeat him and he felt this was a sign of his future. He was ready for battle, and his spirit was intact, ready for what was to come. When he awoke the next morning, there was a tray of food next to his bed and the large steel door was half open. As he crawled off the bed and stood straight and firm, he looked at the door and knew that he had won.

CRY OF FREEDOM

Daniel walked out his door of the second east ward, breathing in freedom. There was a long hallway with a bathroom at the end. It reminded him of his stay in the hospital years before, when he was a child. There were two large wooden doors with silver handles adjacent to the four steel doors. He quietly slipped through one, reaching for a knob but finding a silver handle in his grasp instead. The door led to a larger hallway with rooms that were adjacent to the wooden doors. As he passed these doors and headed toward a room at the end of the hallway, he saw elderly women sitting up in their beds. They had white curly hair and flowery nightgowns. They scowled at him as he went by. He entered the room at the end of the hallway. A passing nurse told him it was the sun room, and that he was to stay out of the older women's rooms. This was a place for socializing, filled with many chairs, but there was no one there. The windows were clear and

e could see foliage growing right outside the
. The sun shown through the windows, warming the room. A nurse came and escorted Daniel back to his room, where their was a tray of food growing cold. The eggs looked like brains to him, and the bacon was like the flesh from a dead person's leg. He refused to eat. The nurse pressured him but he would not. She locked him in the room with the tray of food, and as time passed she would check on him periodically. He thought to himself that he would starve to death before he would eat. Lunchtime came, and the breakfast tray was taken away and another tray placed before him. This one had beets that looked like a bloody mass of tissue, maybe a liver or a heart. A different nurse came in and tested the food for him, but he still refused to eat, wondering what kind of human being she was? She eventually caught on regarding what he was experiencing from the look on his face. She explained to him what each type of food was, reminding him that he had seen these in the past. He understood and carefully tasted the food, ready to spit it out at the first sign of a foul taste. Through his mind ran the thoughts "What if they took body parts and made them taste and look like food? Was this the main objective of hospitals in today's society? Have the hospitals been feeding us human flesh for years without telling us? Are the people

of the earth really starving to death, and upon their deaths becoming the food for the living?" This seemed unholy to Daniel, and he would not allow himself to believe it. He rationalized that his society would not have taught him the values they had and then turn on him like this. This was his first indication that there was something wrong with his thinking. He continued to eat, knowing that he must eat to survive, and felt that if his thoughts proved true he would kill himself and remain faithful to Christ. He saw this as a threat to his belief in Christianity, for Christ may have sacrificed his body, but in no way did he mean for people to literally eat the flesh of others.

When he was through, he went to the sun porch and began to bathe in the afternoon light. He felt waves of peace from above descending onto his head and shoulders and running through his body. As the feeling overcame him, he blocked out all sounds and sights. In the distance he heard a faint cry for help. As he turned his attention to the cry, the feeling of peace began to leave him as it had come, in waves. His mental ability steadily increased and he was able to hold his concentration for longer periods of time.

Daniel had an argument with one of the nurses over something he thought was trivial and was locked in his room. He spoke out through the small grate window but no one paid attention to him. His tongue began to move, flapping up, down, and sideways. All of a sudden, Daniel began speaking in a foreign tongue, which he knew was impossible. Spiritual thoughts began running through his mind and on the angel, who called herself Gabriel. A mental transmission was flowing through his mind. It was Gabriel, telling him of future events he would experience, and of events involving people he knew or would come to know. Daniel knew little or nothing of Gabriel. The name was new to him, or so he thought, and the future events that she spoke of seemed impossible. After about an hour, his mind and tongue tired, and he grew silent in relief. Mentally blank, listening to silence, he laid down, feeling calm because his experience was one of persevering in questioning the quest of his life. He could rest now, assured he would have a difficult and trying life, but that he would also survive to know God. As time passed in his life, events occurred he related to the mental transmissions of the angelic presence.

One day as he was walking up the hall, setting new boundaries and looking into other rooms to see who was in them, he was astounded to see a man who had his leg amputated. It was terribly frightening, and the thought of cannibalism raced through his mind. He walked farther and came to a room which was larger than most, containing several beds. There was an old woman in one bed pressuring him to get the nurse. He did not. He was used to this. He turned and looked at another bed in front of a large picture window containing his mother. Bruised, scarred, and swollen, her skin covered with purple and yellow splotches, she lay on the bed, afflicted by the Lupus she had borne for many years. When she looked at her son, sorrow filled her eyes. When he saw her, his heart fell, and he reciprocated her sorrow, gazing back into her deep blue eyes. She spoke a few words of encouragement to him when a nurse came in and sent him back down the hall where the staff could watch him.

It was Christmas time, and on Christmas he received a package from his mother—a shirt. Around this time one of his brothers and his sister Rose came to see him. Rose was the sister who had brought him here. During their visit, they only frightened him with pressure to get well. He was fully aware that what he was experiencing was incomprehensible to their limited imagination. Several other sisters came to visit Daniel, and one brought her new husband. Daniel saw them briefly but soon excused himself because their motive for coming was curiosity, not to comfort him. A stranger also came to visit. He had a round face, thick skin, and a pot belly. He wore a sports coat and a cap.

His countenance reminded Daniel of God in some way. He was called Jug. Jug visited Daniel and brought books that held spiritual meaning and significance for him. He made an effort to understand Daniel's deeper thoughts and feelings, and Jug asked him to stay at his halfway house for alcoholics when he was released from the hospital. Daniel agreed, for he had nowhere else to go.

THE FAMILY

Newcastle was a dirty old town, filled with worn-out houses and a number of old cars. Due to the oil boom in the state, there were also some new homes. The people whom Daniel would come to know for the greater part of his stay lived, partied, and survived in the poorer parts of town. . He asked someone on main street where he could find his family. As it is in all small towns, everybody in Newcastle knew everyone's business, who they were, and where they lived. A couple of women pointed the way for him; the house was located a couple of blocks off Main Street. When he arrived, he was greeted with surprise, and welcomed by his brother in laws family. That night, the family played cards and discussed his future. He planned to go to school and to work. He asked his brother if he had a room he could use. His brother said yes, but told Daniel he would have to find a job if he wanted to live with him. The next day Daniel's uncle, Ralph, and his grandmother showed up and insisted Daniel come home. There was some arguing and a few promises were made, so he headed back to Casper with them. When he got home, nothing had changed and things got worse. He became the family's target and took potshots from all of them. The arguing and pressure disturbed Daniel so much he went back to Newcastle. Once there, he started school, found a job in a grocery store, bought a pink, tail-finned, push-button Pontiac, and lived with his brother for a short time. His brother threw him out for some strange reason, then the two of them fought physically and Dave won..

Joan's family of girls and no husband, liked Daniel a lot. The former orphan-turned–run-away-kid, half boy and half man, learned to survive on his own, and he went to live in a friend's garage, where he also housed his Pontiac.

He had lived in the garage for a few weeks when two kids at school who had a very small, two-bedroom, heated apartment, asked Daniel to stay with them. In Newcastle, Daniel had his first experiences with loose women and alcohol. He found the students at the high school he attended disliked him. They considered him trouble due to his long hair. The principal made him get a hair cut before he could continue to attend school. It was nearing Christmas again, and one of his sister-in-laws saw him on the street and told him his mother wanted him to call her. Daniel's heart fell. "Maybe she is going to die," he thought. As his mind tried to find answers that seemed to escape him, he headed for a public phone in the town hotel.

Daniel called home and his mother answered. He explained how one of Sandy's—his brother's wife—sisters had told him he should call. His mother was brief and to the point as she always was. "Patty is living with your dad," she explained. "Jack is going back to the Cathedral Home in Laramie after Christmas and will never come home again. Kathy has her own home and baby. Uncle Ralph has left and Grandmother has decided to step out of the picture some. Your step-dad is leaving, and that leaves Rose and I and the four little girls. Rose is starting to get into trouble, and I need you to be the man of the house." She paused. "I'm sick," she continued, "and I don't have much time left, but I hope I can see all my kids grow to be adults. You know how to make the best out of a bad situation, and you are strong—not just physically, but mentally. You have good morals, and I need you now. Think about it and call me. These younger girls need a strong arm if they are going to make it."

Daniel waited three days; he had mixed feelings. He decided his quest for personal adventure and success would have to wait. He called his mother and gave her his word he would do all he could. From that point on, when they talked, there was relief in her voice. He told her about his car, and she sent Jack in an old brown-panel pick-up truck to help pull it back to town. Jack and a couple of friends with long hair who wore hippie clothes came and chained the pink Pontiac to the truck. As they were heading down the highway, Ed Dakota, an Indian riding with Daniel, punched a button, put the car into gear, and started the car. Jack pulled over when he saw the lights flashing behind him. Both Ed and Daniel then unhitched the car from the truck and took turns driving down the road. Ed told spirited Indian stories while Daniel listened intently. The two of them also discussed Daniel's future with the family and Ed promised to help Daniel if he was ever in need. Daniel went home for a couple years to help his mother, and as it turned out, he made many friends. He had two years left in school during which he would not see Ed Dakota again.

THE DREAM

By now, Daniel's reddish-brown hair flowed down to his lower back. His brother Dave, had a friend who had a request. Karl, Dave's friend, and his wife, Judy, wanted Daniel to stay with Judy, who was pregnant while Karl was in Vietnam. Karl had been drafted into the Army. Daniel was to see that things between his home with his sisters and mother, and Judy were good. When Karl returned and checked with Daniel, everything was fine. Daniel spent one night alone at Karl and Judy's home.

That night while Judy was gone, Daniel fell asleep on the floor with the TV on. He had an incredible dream. It was about the immediate family of God, which included twenty-four children, God, and Gabriel. There were three young male adults missing. These were Michael, Emanuel, and Daniel. Their positioning was unique. There was a place for one to the right, one to the left, and one in front of the Ancient of Days, who had flowing white hair and a beard. He sat in his large, white stone chair. To the left of the Ancient One was a woman holding a child over a stream which flowed out before the throne. Her name was Gabriel. On the other side of the stream were two younger women, and one held the mate to the other child being held over the stream.

Below Gabriel and to her left were the rest of the children. They sat in pairs in a line, wearing matching clothes and holding instruments or other small items to identify themselves. Of these children, there were three pairs directly in the center of the row. Two were African, two were Oriental, and two were Indian. These three represented Mohammad, Confucius, and Buddha, while the one being held over the stream was Moses. All the others were Caucasian.

There was one more person, a young woman who stood behind a wooden alter to the left of the Ancient of Days. Carved into the alter were images of lions, words, and all laid upon it were weapons of various kinds, including a bow and spear. The names were as follows: The Whelp of the Lion, The War Lion, The Lion of Judah, and The Lion of Zion. All of them had what is known as the spirit of the lion. Daniel contemplated the dream for many days and had difficulty sleeping until he came to an understanding regarding its meaning, which would increase over time. This is a mystery only dreamers can understand, or maybe Prophets. Daniel knew these things were spiritual in nature, and he was a spiritual person.

BACK TO THE FAMILY

At this point in time, the personalities of the family members had achieved a certain stability. The family broke into small groups. The four younger sisters developed an alliance amongst themselves for the purpose of protection. Daniel's sister Rose attempted to work with the younger girls, teaching them cooking and cleaning skills, because she saw their futures as being bleak. Daniel was in his last year of high school, and he and his friends got into pot. Rose was attractive and had many friends.

She was helpful, but due to the circumstances, she took a lot of guff from her grandmother. It seemed like she could not do enough. Rose and her grandmother Florence had periodic wars. Rose left home, she married Butch, a Vietnam veteran, who married her with the stipulation that when she was of legal age they would divorce. She was seventeen. It was either marriage or the Sheridan State Training Girls School. After her divorce when she was nineteen, Rose lived with her brother Daniel for awhile. Shortly thereafter, she married a man called Mal, a Midwestern parts salesman who transferred to Wyoming to work for his mother. The marriage lasted about six years and produced two children—Jason and Mandy. Rose found out that Mal was unfaithful. After taking time for herself, she married a man called Sam, and they had a daughter. They were a happing family, the three children and Sam and Rose. They built themselves a construction company. Rose admired Daniel and told him what a wonderful life he lived.

Patti's life was another case. She was more family-oriented than the rest of the family. She wanted to be her mother's helper and the mother at the same time. She was torn between family and self. Daniel could see that she was trying. The rest of the family saw how she tried to hold the family together.

Daniel learned from Patti's mistakes, since he was also trying to hold the family together, but for a different reason. He saw the family as a whole, marching through life together. It was like a war with casualties and death soon to come. He held on, not for the sake of the family but for humanity. Patti started college, met a young man from Pennsylvania named Jim, married, and became a homemaker. She promised her mother she would help her stepsisters grow up. Diana, Dawn, Maiva, and Waiva, the four younger girls, found themselves bound to trouble at different times in their lives, even as adults. Patti helped in an authoritarian style.

Each year for Christmas she would invite the entire family over, as this was a special time for her—more so than any other in her life. She shared her home, and her motherhood and sisterhood, and she was always ready to give her input in any given situation. She equated success with how her Christmas turned out because her mother had always been so good at it, and she was forever trying to be like her mom in some ways.

Kathy and Dave ignored the family. They were busy pursuing working interests outside the home. Both of them worked for their Uncle Carl for a while, and Kathy ended up with a career with a telephone company, where she became an executive. Dave followed the drilling rigs from Wyoming to New Mexico, and to Saudi Arabia and back. When hard times hit Wyoming, he sold wood with Jack and Daniel, and finally just with Daniel. When there was not enough money, he went to California and sought help from his dad. Dave's father helped him get established in driving heavy equipment vehicles, and introduced him to Los Angeles. Dave was reckless, and he drank and smoked pot. His recklessness cost him many jobs and a great deal of money. A scorecard could have been kept on the number of cars and motorcycles he wrecked, as well as on his traffic tickets.

Kathy was into religion. She became a teacher of her religion, which was called Unity. She often sent cards and books to the rest of the family, but Daniel saw it all as wishful thinking. Her son, Chris, and her other son, Mike, found no interest in it. Mike became a born-again Christian, while Chris listened to acid rock and followed satanic cults. Chris had his own Dungeons and Dragon's game with metal figures which he painted, and he thought they gave him some type of evil power. Kathy and Dave never had too much to do with the family in Casper, Wyoming, but from time to time they would come around or ask Daniel to come visit them.

THE VISION

Jug drove Daniel to his new residence in December of 1972 after he was released from the hospital. It was a red brick building, and the sign in front read, "Well Being". The snow was deep and everything was bright, even at night. As Daniel entered the large brick house, there were several old, wrinkled men there to greet him. Jug asked one of them—a greasy, curly, black-haired, short man who walked with a limp—to show him where he would be staying.

He was taken down a long, carpeted hallway covered with pictures and passed a long dining room and a large kitchen, and came upon a stairway. The short man led the way down the stairs to a huge room. It was a basement with small windows and about a dozen beds. No one was there. There was a laundry room off the foot of the stairs and a bathroom, which he was shown. The bathroom contained two metal showers with shower curtains that faced two toilets. The bathroom was in the shape of an "L," and as one exits, they pass the showers and three sinks with three mirrors. The door had a full-length mirror on it as well. Everything in the bathroom was white, including the walls. As they exited the bathroom, the short man said, "Pick any bed." Daniel realized no one else was staying in the basement, and he wondered where the old men stayed. He later found out they stayed in private rooms that were upstairs above the central floor. Daniel spent a great deal of time in the basement alone. He investigated every corner of the room. On the card table at one end of the room, someone was putting together a puzzle that bore the likeness of Christ's face. The puzzle was far from complete. Daniel decided if he was going to stay here, the room and everything in it would have to be cleaned. He cleaned the room, and made the beds, swept the floor, wiped everything down, and washed every loose piece of cloth he found as well. He did an immaculate job on the bathroom.

His cleaning spree took several days. He ate with the old men and read the book Jug gave him (*The Prophet* by Kahlil Gibran) in the drawing room. Afterward he returned to the den in the basement. Night fell, and he was satisfied everything was clean and all his responsibilities were accomplished. He walked into the bathroom with one towel and no washcloth. He first turned on the hot water and soaked the heat in; the December chill was on. He slowly turned the hot water down and turned up the cold. The room filled with steam, and he saw this as having a cleansing effect on the room and himself. Stepping out of the shower, he dried his strong muscular body and long reddish brown hair with his towel. Wrapping the towel around his waist, he passed the three mirrors and stopped in front of the door with the full-length mirror.

As he looked into the mist, he became aware of a figure coming toward him—a beautiful, ancient man in a white stone chair. Soon the room was filled with more than mist. It also contained a feeling of exaltation. The ancient one disappeared, and before him stood a man who was clothed in white linen; his arms hung next to his body and his palms were open, facing Daniel. Neither of them spoke, but Daniel detected knowledge was being transferred to himself from the brightly shining omnipotent man with the white hair and lightening eyes. He did not know how long he had been standing there. The glorious one before him was suspended a couple of feet in the air in order to signify royalty and height above the young man. This being, who came and went like lightning, left Daniel standing in amazement in the mist. When he regained his composure, the God-like figure was gone. He took the brass handle of the doorknob and pushed the door open to see if anyone was in the huge room. No one was. In his head, he heard a voice reassuring him and explaining things to him. The same thought entered his mind over and over again: "I am that I am." Daniel lay on his bed, looking at the clock; he realized he had been in the bathroom for about three and a half hours. Faith was his only expectation for these spiritual events. Daniel had no choice but to believe.

Daniel closed his eyes to recall what he had seen, and fell asleep. The next morning he had new energy, which the older men seemed to pick up on. One tall, thin man with a long face picked on him about his long hair and said several times, "Who do you think you are with that long hair, Jesus Christ?" Daniel ignored him and the rest of the elderly men and confined himself to his book and to the basement.

That night three of his friends from school—Mike, Marty, and Jamie—came by to visit. As they were coming down the stairs, Daniel envisioned them wearing robes that were almost as bright as the robes in the vision he had witnessed the previous night. His friends' robes were clean, but they had long cuts in them, as if swords had cut them. The cuts were on the sleeves and lower parts of the robes. Daniel turned away from them in fear. What he saw was ominous. While sitting at the card table, he was astonished to see the puzzle that bore the likeness of Christ was nearly finished, missing only a few pieces. The thought that his vision had surely been of Christ crossed his mind at that instant. Maybe it really happened and it was not a vision at all. The three young men came up behind Daniel and tried to persuade him to go with them. He would not, so Jamie chose to stay and spend some time talking to him, giving him comfort and companionship. The following day Daniel walked about a mile to his mother's house through the cold and snow. He had a compelling desire to tell her of his experience. She had been released from the hospital about the same time he had. When he got to her home, she was alone. His younger sisters had been sent to their older sister Patti's home. His mother was lying on the couch, wearing a green nightgown, with a cigarette in her hand and an old blue blanket wrapped around her. Her black hair was thin and combed straight, and it contained grey streaks. Her face was aged beyond her years and her body was thin, weak, and frail. Margret had been her son's most respected and beloved authority. She had been stricken, and brought down to where she now was physically and mentally exhausted. She looked as though she were in her ninety's, but she was actually only thirty-nine. She had been a good mother to him, and had been his strength when he was weak. Now his strength would be hers.

Daniel began to tell her of his vision. As he spoke, her eyes followed him around the room. He stood by a bookshelf full of books that she had read. She smiled, with an understanding look in her eyes, and then for a moment, as he paused, she gave him a serious look. It was in that moment, they both knew she would soon be gone. He went on talking for a short time and then quit. Ready to leave, he put on his old army coat he had been wearing for several years now and told her to call if she needed anything. She nodded and sent him off with a smile.

The next morning his grandmother called and asked him to come to his mother's house. She wanted him to carry his battle-weary mother to the car so she could be taken back to the hospital. He ran and walked, until he got to the house. She was worse off than she had been the day before, and he and his grandmother wrapped his mother in a blanket. Daniel picked her up in his arms and, as his soul cried out, carried her to the car. He watched them drive off, and when they were gone he walked down the street with a tear in his eye.

The following days were tense, and at the suggestion of a friend, Daniel took his mother a dozen roses. This was the last time he would see her alive. She lay in bed in pain and agony as the medications became useless. One morning Mary Kathryn, his oldest sister, came and sat alone with him in Jug's chambers, telling him of his mother's death. He was grief stricken but did not care to share this with his sister, who made a vain attempt to council and comfort him. He needed time to be alone. For the next few weeks he mourned.

HELL

While Daniel was in the hospital, a doctor prescribed medication for him. The psychiatrist told him he had better take it, but she wasn't sure for how long. She suggested that he should see her on a regular basis. Daniel took the prescriptions in his hand. He failed to take the medications. This was a mistake. In the beginning he noticed no change at all. Jug wanted him to get a job and pay his way, implying he would not always be allowed to stay there.

Daniel took a job at WATCO, a welding company. There he swept floors covered with metal shavings that looked like hundreds of corkscrews of all shapes and sizes. As he pushed the broom, he began to feel paranoid. He suffered from fear his fellow workers might be of an evil nature. His mind became confused, and instead of glorious visions and immaculate feelings, he felt like he was on the verge of disaster after only a couple weeks. Nothing much had happened yet, but he sensed something fearful would happen—and it did.

Daniel's brother Jack visited one night and convinced Daniel he should leave Well Being and join his brothers, who were working in an oil field in Utah. The following day, after collecting his check from WATCO, the two of them packed Daniel's things in the car and headed for Vernal, Utah. Jack drove the icy highway at night, down the snow covered mountains, while Daniel's fears began to swell. He started talking incoherently to Jack, who made an effort to understand his mentally ill brother. Jack began to wonder if he had done the right thing, but it was too late to turn back. They had gone too far, and Jack had to be to work in the morning. Jack left Daniel in his other brother David's room in Vernal, Utah. Jack then left for Duchene, Utah where he lived and worked. Dave was working on a drilling rig somewhere in the Utah plains.

Daniel's room had two double beds and a bathroom. There was a chess game set up between the beds that someone had been playing. A small color TV sat in a corner of the bedroom by a window, and there was a book sitting on the windowsill. Daniel went to the window and picked it up curiously because he knew his brother David did not read. He began reading the book. It was called the Book of Mormon. After reviewing it, he decided it was not for him. A few days later, Dave took Daniel to the Wyoming State Hospital after seeing Daniel could hardly understand him. There, he was locked in a cell with a heavy metal door, behind a door half as thick. He prayed every night and every morning, asking who he was, why he was there, and what his future would be. One morning, an unknown woman came in to let him out for breakfast; she hurried out the heavy metal door. Daniel was still on his knees, and upon rising, he headed for the outside door, but his name was called just as he reached it. It was a loud and powerful voice. A similar thing happened after he was let out and moved to a new unit. There he walked in a hallway which was, amazingly, empty. The patients and staff all had gone to lunch, and Daniel, trying to pray for understanding, heard the roar of a magnificent lion. What he had heard had came from above. He experienced a few other miraculous events at that time, but they are more personal, to be told another time. After the hospital he went to work.

P. A. INCORPORATED

P.A. was a pipe inspectors' company. Daniel learned the tools of the trade rather quickly. His Indian boss named him "Lightning" because of the way he moved. He became the outside lead man and trained many a hand. Just when he got to know and handle a crew, they were replaced and he was given some new worms. A worm is what they call someone new to the oil field. One new crew, along with Loren, his boss, and Daniel were called out to do a job near Cody, Wyoming out on the prairie. The wind was gusting at up to seventy miles an hour. The temperature was below zero and small flakes of snow blew across the plains off and on.

The crew started Sunday afternoon, and evening. They were working on twelve inch casing, which is about as big a pipe as you can find. The thirty-foot pipe was heavy and hard to move.

Late that night, the crew was complaining about

the wind and cold. Nothing can interrupt you when a pipe has to be put down the hole. Daniel kept pushing the hands until they finally folded and quit.

Daniel talked to Loren, and he informed Daniel to tell the worms, they weren't leaving until the job was done.

Loren came out of the warm unit and started to kick the pipe as far up on the pipe rack as he could get it. Daniel got the worms warmed up in the truck, and he told them no one was going anywhere, until the job was done, and anyone who didn't work wouldn't be getting a ride home, and would have to walk out in the wind and cold. He told them to make their decision regarding whether they would work or walk home, and that in five minutes he was going back out there. What Daniel told them worked and all the men came out shortly after he did. Loren was done stacking the pipe. The next day, Monday, at about noon, the job was finished, the trucks were loaded, and the crew, including Loren, headed for Thermopolis. Elmer who drove the truck and trailor drank a lot off work. He drove the truck and trailor which could inspect the pipe for pits and cracks. He was what was called a lifer. It was amazing how he could park the truck on the perfect spot. On the way to Thermopolis everyone fell asleep as Daniel was driving. Daniel dozed off, and was awakened when the truck started to go off the road. He woke up, but since no one else did, he forced himself to stay awake and drove the crew safely to Thermopolis, where he went to a motel room and crashed. He woke up five hours later and everybody got steaks. Then they headed back to Casper, with Daniel driving again.

The next morning they had the day off, and they were scheduled to go back out in two days. The crew was to meet at the restaurant that morning, but the only people to show up were Lauren and Lightning. It was going to take a while to get a new crew. After four days, a new crew was ready to head toward Buffalo, Wyoming. Daniel was beginning to become confused because his medicine was not working. He would have to leave to get help.

The job was at a drill site, and the crew stayed in a motel in Buffalo. Daniel talked with Lauren, and Lauren asked if he would come back. Lightning said he would if he could. Daniel caught a bus in Buffalo to Casper and drove to the Wyoming State Hospital. He stayed there for three months while his medication was adjusted, and then he went back to work for PA Incorporated. They sent him to Williston, North Dakota, and began training him to be an operator.

Daniel's best friend, Jamie, died in a truck rollover in which five people, including the driver, fell asleep because of smoking pot. They were all Daniel's friends but it was his best friend who had died. Daniel's heart was broken, and he was getting tired of traveling, so he walked off the job with another fellow and caught a bus home after being there a month. Daniel didn't work again for several weeks. He ended up getting counseling, which he gravely needed.

NEXT STOP WYOMING MACHINERY CO.

Daniel managed to get an interview at the Wyoming Machinery Co. The man conducting the interview hired him right on the spot. Two weeks after, he began working for Wyoming Machinery Co. This was in December of 1977. Daniel struggled to fill orders in the parts building. He had to learn the system. There seemed to be millions of parts, ranging from very small to very large. Practically everything was metal, though a few parts were made of rubber or plastic.

He caught on after a while. He became fast and precise. One thing about Daniel, there wasn't any job he could not learn to do; even though he could not keep a job for more than a year and a half at that time, due to his illness. This kept him poor, and he lived in poverty, in what might be described as living in shacks. Every time he got sick, his money would soon be gone, and so would his housing, if you could call it that.

While he worked at the Wyoming Machin
he lived in a dilapidated apartment. He helped the
company move to a newer building and worked his
way up to being the parts return man. He would work
with parts that were small or large or in between, and
he would have to find the number for it and its original cost. The accountant would make the adjustment,
and whichever mine had sent it would be reimbursed.
He would use microfiche to do his work. There were
millions of descriptions and numbers, and just like
he could learn any job, he could look at parts, large or
small, and know what category they fell under. Before
Daniel left the Wyoming Machinery Co., he missed
a doctor's appointment and had no way of getting his
medication. The doctor called his job and told his boss
he should be laid off until he got it. His boss, who hired
him, told him he needed to quit, so he did.

Now he had no job, no money, and no medication,
and in a short amount of time he was very ill.

Then some strange things happened. Daniel moved
from a shack in Mountain View, Wyoming to a small
trailer in Evansville, Wyoming. Both towns were small,
rural, and bordered Casper, Wyoming. Daniel had no
choice but to accept the life he led. He couldn't get a
good paying job and he bordered on poverty.

Daniel was very ill at this time, and he spent a

month at the state hospital in Evanston, Wyoming. Prior to this, he went to Cheyenne, Wyoming straight to a bar, walked in, and looked for an old friend named Suzy. He could not find her. He had not seen her for many years, and had not called her because he did not have her phone number. What drew him to that particular bar is any body's guess. As he had a beer, he sat and wondered what had he done. He decided to shoot pool, and took a couple shots. The bar door then blew open, and amazingly Suzy came in, went over by the bar stools, and then came to him. Something powerful came over Daniel. The last time he had seen Suzy was in 1973 at the Wyoming State Hospital, and she had a spiritual white mark. They talked briefly, and she asked him to go home, but not before asking how he had gotten there. He told her that he had stolen his brother's car. Daniel never considered this meeting to be a coincidence; he saw it as another act of God. After all, he saw a round, white mark on her left cheek, just like the color he had seen on his friends clothing, many years ago at 'Well Being' during the onset of his illness and his growing awareness of his own spirituality.

Daniel and Suzy parted ways again to never to see each other again. Still, there had been a connection. Daniel left Cheyenne, and returned to Casper, his brother was angry about his having stolen the car.

It was subsequently decided Daniel should g~ state hospital, so he went. Daniel went willingly because there was something about Suzy in all of this. The state hospital put him back on medication. They put structure back in his life as they always did, and then sent him back to Casper.

Upon his return to Casper, having had thoughts about spiritual words and names which often occurred, many other events were confusing and disabled him from working. Also, the remembrance of visions, voices, and dreams graced his mind. These were spiritual in nature, and not based in Daniel's illness, for that is negative and confusing. These experiences were spiritually real and certainly powerful. Their direction was forward, honest, and clear. To the observer, they cannot be denied or forgotten. These kinds of things catapult individuals into another dimension.

It may be that illness, confusion, and negativity have to be balanced, and therefore that which is balanced is spiritual. Like the scales of justice, which are evenly balanced, with confusion and negativity on one side and spirituality and absolute truth on the other, it is only through balance, sanity achieves its full measure and weight.

In other words, true spirituality cannot be denied because it creates its own reality and is more powerful than anything else in the universe. It will not be forgotten or changed. This is only a part of the same inexhaustible spirituality he knew.

THE BLACK SHEEP

Daniel later got out of the state hospital and came back to Casper, where he rented a room in a dirty, filthy motel housing mostly drunks. Daniel had been there one day when an old man called the office of the motel about needing cement work done. Daniel went and did the work for him. Since Daniel had Social Security money coming in, the old man offered him a room in his basement.

Daniel had some friends who were Jehovah Witnesses, and they spent about a year trying to rope him in to their religion. One of the witnesses gave Daniel a job cleaning an office. This occurred when Daniel was living in the basement, and also later when he lived in a shack. He also found work cleaning laundromats.

Daniel was in the hospital prior to this, having his medications changed, which had been recommended by his counselor. When Daniel got back from the hospital, his psychiatrist had been charged for sexual harassment, among other things; he was having sexual relations with the female clients. However, he wanted Daniel to take some time off work.

Daniel moved a couple of times to places that were unfit for human habitation. His brothers, Jack and Dave, wanted him to work with them, gathering firewood on the mountain next to Casper. Daniel was paid very little, and Dave would not pay him at all most of the time. He said he needed the money for his family. Daniel was treated like the black sheep of the family. They had him splitting and throwing the wood. This was the hardest part of the job. Daniel was quite poor, and his brothers treated him with disrespect.

While Daniel worked for Jack and Dave, his counselor got him into HUD housing. This was very nice, and was better than any place he had ever lived. Unfortunately, the hard work and summer heat caused him to have a minor stroke. Daniel's right eyelid drooped, partially covering his eye, and the right side of his mouth was turned down. To recover from these effects, Daniel did a lot of reading and gum chewing. It worked for the most part. However, it never completely went back to normal. Shortly after this, he quit.

BROTHERS LOST
IN THE STORM

J ack was more and more insistent each day that Daniel should help him work the firewood. He came over one day and said, "Karen is leaving and taking the kids." Karen was Jack's wife. Daniel tried to understand what Jack was going through, but never having had a wife or children himself, he was at a loss for words. Daniel had quit and Jack was in a bind. Karen did leave, taking the children with her back to where she was raised—Williston, North Dakota. Jack grew more and more distant; he sat at Daniel's house in a daze. At times, he would come up with schemes for getting his children back. One time he plotted with Daniel to steal his son Justin and take him across the Montana border before anyone could find out. Jack left for a few days and later turned up with Justin. The little boy seemed confused and frightened, but he had his father's determination and seemed ready to stick it out. Jack tried to take care of Justin, but he began to realize he could not do it. When money ran out, as well as his options for places to stay, he took Justin back to Williston. Karen eventually sent him divorce papers, which he refused to sign.

Daniel talked Jack into going to California to see their dad because he thought it might help. No such luck. Jack stayed for a few days by using credit cards his dad had given to him, but he was dissatisfied with Los Angeles. He returned to Casper, explaining to Daniel their dad had not been much help. Daniel became worried because his brother had ceased to work, and he wanted to borrow money. He expected Daniel to feed him. Daniel suggested that he go to Cheyenne to see his sister, Kathy. Daniel felt inadequate because he was at a loss for what to do. Referring to Daniel's illness, Jack asked him, "Could what happened to you happen to me?"

"No," Daniel replied. "You're too old. And besides, if what happened to me happens to you, you will know it."

Jack drove his brown two-ton pickup truck with wooden side rails down to Cheyenne. Kathy greeted him with open arms. She gave him run of the house while she was at work, and also while she was out of town on a business trip. When she had gone, Jack called Daniel and told him that he felt like ending his life. Jack had threatened this once before, his sister told him.

This time was different. Karen was not coming back, and Jack was steadily losing his mind. Daniel suspected his brother was experiencing the same ill effects that he had years before. He called the police in Cheyenne, but their reply was, "If he asks us for help we can give it to him, but if not, there's nothing we can do." They went to the house and Jack told them he was not in need of their help. When Daniel called them back, they repeated what they had said earlier. Jack called Daniel back, and this time there was no mincing of words. Jack asked timidly, "Is there anything I could do that would cause God not to love me?"

Daniel's reply was, "No, God is so great that you really don't have control over his love. Anything you might do or not do does not change his love for you." Daniel knew what his brother was saying. He was contemplating suicide. Daniel knew if he had told his brother God did not love him he would have put his brother into a position that would have made the situation worse, if that were possible. The police could not help, and after Daniel hung up the phone, a sick feeling came into his stomach because he knew he had lost his brother. A couple of days later, after many phone calls, their sister, Kathy, came home. She found Jack's body in his truck. It was somewhat deformed because he had been there a few days, having died of asphyxiation. The services were held in Casper, and Kathy had Jack's remains in a small container after she had the body cremated. The entire family came to the funeral. Karen came with suspicions. She thought Jack had something up his sleeve, and it was just a trick, though she was not quite sure. She left convinced Jack's death was not just a trick after she saw his ashes. The boy who wanted to succeed had been reduced to a pile of ashes that were scattered over the snow-covered Casper Mountain by his sister, his wife, and his friends.

Several months later, another tragedy beset Daniel's family. This time it was Chris, who was Daniel's nephew—Kathy's son. Chris was in high school and he had begun to use drugs. He was also interested in hard rock and roll, and a game called Dungeons and Dragons. Chris collected pieces to the game and painted them. They were small figurines made out of metal. He meticulously painted his collection. Chris was experiencing hallucinations, thought to be caused by drugs, and was sent to an out-of-state hospital for help. The doctors at the hospital decided his problems were not caused by drugs, but by schizophrenia. Chris never adjusted to the illness, and after much debate, he went to live with his father, who did not believe he had a problem at all. This complicated the situation. He was depressed following his mother's refusal to let him come home for the holidays, and to spend time with his friends. During his final visits Chris and Daniel talked about God, whom Chris had rejected earlier. Daniel's religious values were similar to Jack's before he died. Like the thief on the cross, in the last moments in their lives, Jack, and now Chris, embraced Christianity. It was not long before Chris killed himself with a shotgun. With Jack and Chris gone, Daniel felt the family had lost two great individuals. To his knowledge, they had harmed no one, although they were expected to do so. They left a void in Daniel, a void that would later be filled by his education and future life experiences.

For about ten years Daniel knew the terror of this illness and what it could do. It was a miracle he was alive. He felt sorrow for his brothers in his heart, but he knew very few people could have lived through what he had. It's a terrible thing to possess the knowledge that the illness that had attacked his family had killed his brother and his nephew. Most people realize cancer is a killer, but few people realize schizophrenia—an inherited disease—is also potentially fatal. Daniel also knew there was little protection out there, against his illness and at times he wished he had cancer instead. He felt it would be better to suffer and die from Lupus than it would be to continually suffer from his schizophrenia. Some of his dreams dealt with this possibility. He thought he might get lucky and get the Lupus his mother had. At the very least it would give him an honorable way out. This was all about to change, however, because Daniel's life was about to take an interesting turn.

Daniel had met some interesting people through his counselor at the Central Wyoming Counseling Center. Jim, whom he had been associated with for a year, consulted with Daniel regarding the idea of starting a group to help people with chronic mental illness. Daniel knew people in his predicament needed help, and he listened intently as Jim described what other family members of people with this illness and those suffering from it had done in other states. Daniel was charged up by Jim's talk, and he pursued the idea by attending various meetings. He found a group of people with whom he felt partially accepted. He made efforts to prove himself sane and worthy over and over again, and he soon found he was trusted and respected. His goal was more than to find a way to help himself; it became a crusade to help others whom he knew were suffering, or who would some day suffer.

Three people who took special interest in Daniel were Marge, Herb, and Bob. Daniel's family took little interest in the Family Alliance for the Mentally Ill. However, about a year before Chris and Jack's death, his sister Kathy had become the president of a similar group in Cheyenne. After the first year, the group in Cheyenne began to dissolve, but a new group for the whole state was being formed. It would be called the Wyoming Alliance for the Mentally Ill.

After losing Jack and Chris, the whole idea of a group became a quest for Daniel. He had nothing to lose and everything to gain. He could make simple mistakes that would simply be overlooked and classified in the category of mental illness. However, after Daniel attained achievement after achievement, he brought honor to those who suffered. Daniel was extremely bright and looked at his quest as if he were going to war. If he died, he would be a hero, and if he lived, he would be able to see that things would only get better for him and those like him. He pulled out all the stops and opened himself up to the public like an animal which had been dissected for people to look at in order that they might learn the truth and gain understanding. He took what seemed to him to be God-awful risks and outwardly exposed all of himself for the sake of his people. He gave speeches and attended meetings, feeling at times like he was a lunch-counter protester in Alabama. He left himself wide open to criticism and to instruction. The one question he came to hate, "How do you feel?" still burns his ears to this day.

Because of what he had done, everyone became his analyst and prescribed different types of emotional, mental, and psychological remedies. Daniel was used to this, though. His family had done the same thing to him for years. It seemed to Daniel he was saner than his public thought, as time went by. For who among them had experienced what he had? How many of these so-called well-read authorities ever hope to achieve anywhere near what this young man, had. Who saw him rise spiritually as part lion, part man...His inner strength was great.

Daniel looked at where he had come from and where he was going. Nothing could stop his drive to succeed in his quest. "To dream the impossible dream, to fight the unbeatable foe", a song he had learned and sung in a school play, described what Daniel was all about. When he remembered the words of Martin Luther King, which replayed again and again throughout his life, he gained strength. Unlike racism, however, Daniel knew the cause of his problem was his inner self, and it was not derived from external sources, though the external sources did play a part in the form of the stigma of mental illness attached to his friends and family alike. He saw this stigma as being akin to racism, and he felt the injustice of a thousand slaves and the persecution of his kind through the ages. Daniel had become the War Lion, campaigning against incredible odds and ignorance. For the next five years, he battled the legislature in a passive way. He and his associates, Marge, the mother of a mentally ill daughter, and Bob, who had two mentally ill sons, spoke to representatives of the state. They called themselves the three musketeers. Bob became president of the Family Alliance and later served on the advisory board of the Protection and Advocacy Agency. Marge was a secretary for the Family Alliance and the Wyoming Alliance for the Mentally Ill. Marge was in charge of writing a monthly newsletter for these two groups. Daniel, who served on the board of the Family Alliance, wrote articles with the consumer of mental health services in mind. One of Daniel's articles was published in *The Star-Tribune* in Casper, Wyoming on Wednesday, March 23, 1988, on page A-11. This is what he wrote:

MUST HOMELESS BEG IN ORDER TO BE SEEN??

By DANIEL MEYERS

*W*ill homelessness be construed as a state or federal responsibility? Two or three thousand homeless in Wyoming would like to know. The verdict is still out and will be indefinitely, if some have their way. The pertinent question is whether or not to aid the homeless. We may see policies similar to that of the Elizabethan Poor Law take effect if the country remains wedded to Protestant work-ethic standards.

On Jan. 6, President Reagan signed his first major housing bill. The bill would end temporary suspension of FHA mortgage programs beneficial to young families. The bill also helps the poor to attain rentals with government vouchers. These rentals are sorely needed.

In the past eight years no major housing assistance has come through via pork-barrel amendments to the immigration and seat belt laws.

The issue of homelessness stands between housing and employment. Robert Hayes of the New York–based coalition for the homeless states, "The three-word solution is: Housing, Housing, Housing." The opponent of this issue is James Starks of the Dallas Life Foundation. He would fit in tightly with the Reagan Administration, since he states, "What's needed are jobs and training."

On Feb. 4, 1970, Mayor Richard Daly of Chicago gave several reasons for a deteriorating housing market: Increasing interest rates, higher construction costs, scarcity of materials, and the propensity of contractors to build homes in the more affluent suburbs than in the city. The situation has deteriorated further in the 80's. The number of assisted rental units has gone down from 220,500 in 1981 to less than 98,000 in 1987. There seems to be little change from debates and band aid politics.

Progress has been made recently due to a weakening in the Reagan administration. Sen. Al Gore of Tennessee, candidate for the presidency of the United States, has supported this legislation. HR 5140 with a $4 billion budget made possible a new law which requires the Secretaries of Health and Human Services and Agriculture to develop a single application for SSI and food stamps. These services are to be made available to mental health and penal institutions, to insure the individuals will not be put on the streets without regular support.

I feel this is a major step in thwarting homelessness and re-institutionalization. I was released from the Wyoming State Hospital in 1976 with no home to go to, a month's supply of medicine for a chronic illness, $25, and a bus ticket to Casper. I was one of a few that survived this process, so I have been told. I do not know anyone else who did. I can appreciate this portion of the bill more than most.

Other progressive measures include the right of homeless to pay homeless shelters and soup kitchens with their food stamps. The Emergency Food and Shelter Act was funded with $70 million. In 1982, this was the only money allocated for the homeless.

Gov. Mike Sullivan, recently confronted by the plight of the homeless states, "We'll attempt to do what we can." The same Star-Tribune *article, "Homeless problem even in small Wyoming towns," by Scott Farris, Jan 3, 1988, stated some Wyoming social workers doubt the existence of a homeless problem in Wyoming.*

Wyoming has done little for the homeless and the only visible help is Soul's Anchor in Casper and a homeless center in Jackson. The center in Jackson requires that a person have at least a minimum wage job to stay there. Some federal funds are received by Soul's Anchor. Wyoming is a cold and unpopulated place and if the homeless are gathering here, they are gathering in multitudes in the larger cities of the country. With little financial aid, there is no way to alter the effects of homelessness. The outcome could be wide-spread disease and violence or possibly a massive die-off of the homeless.

The protestant work ethic basically states you get what you earn. Work and you will be rewarded justly. If this is true, then why does the unemployed homeless oilfield hand not have enough to eat? He created wealth for his state and in return, the state has no plan to help him in his time of need. How many legislators own oil stock which benefited from this man's labor?

The Reagan administration and many others imply, "Get a job and you'll have a home." Sharon Shore, Director of the Casper Housing Authority, does not agree. Problems such as low wages, sub-standard housing, and poor economic conditions dispel the Protestant work-ethic myths. The 2,000 to 3,000 homeless people in Wyoming are also apt to disagree. However, there are some Wyoming social workers who feel the problem is not all that serious.

It took only one unfortunate man to draw the Good Samaritan's attention. Two to three thousand homeless should draw the attention of Wyoming social workers. This causes me to question if these people know what field they are in.

In the last quarter of the 20th century, we need to do better than the Elizabethan Poor Law of 1601, where institutionalization began only because people were begging, not because they were poor, ill or homeless. The Elizabethan

Poor Law was instituted not because homeless persons were poor or ill but because they began to beg. This was outrageous to the upper classes. Aid was given to stop the begging. Is this the next phase of the homeless for America?

I feel the Reagan administration has failed in handling such social issues as the homeless. The Wyoming state government is unsure about homelessness. The little aid given here and there is a band aid approach to a bleeding jugular. Some wish to help with jobs, but where are they? Some want to use welfare, but no one wants to pay for it.

The Regan administration turned its back on the homeless. The homeless situation is being debated with no clearcut answers. As long as this debate continues, there will be little aid for the homeless.

The debate had been going on since the 1930's when Franklin D. Roosevelt was president. Sixty years have passed and there is still no solution, only a brief respite during the Johnson administration (the Great Society, in the '60s). It makes one question the effectiveness of the American political system. In 15 years there will be an estimated 19 million homeless in America. The problem is bad and becoming worse. Action is needed now!

(Daniel Meyers is a Casper College student. He is a member of the Wyoming Alliance and the Family Alliance for the Mentally Ill.)

Daniel found success through his efforts. He gained respect and support from friends and professionals. The Casper hospital used him as a type of volunteer ombudsman. He would see clients who had experienced chronic mental illness and would counsel them on the techniques to help them achieve success. He broke these down to eating right, sleeping right, medication management, professional help, and helpful friends. His experience as an orphan, a stepchild, a good student, a poor student, a worker, and a self-educated expert on mental illness—having been diagnosed with schizophrenia and having lived as a mentally ill person made him a valuable asset to the mental health system of Wyoming, and possibly to the country. With all this in mind, Daniel operated in his state for the benefit of families and persons with mental illnesses. One day, Marge asked him if he would go see a new consumer of mental health services. He accepted. She told him a young girl called Vicky would meet with him.

When Daniel pulled up to the house, he saw an obese woman on the right side of the road. He wondered how she would fit in the car. Just then, a short, cute, nicely built, blond woman came to the street, waving her arms and smiling. She later became his wife.

EDUCATION AND EXPERIENCES

Daniel got a letter in the mail from the Department of Vocational Rehabilitation from a woman named Kathy Cassidy. She talked with him about going to school, but said he would have to be tested first. A psychiatrist named Jacque Herder gave Daniel some tests consisting of inkblots, math, grammar, evaluations, and so forth. He said after the testing Daniel could go to school for a couple of years and he could get a better job. When he saw Kathy, she wanted him to try it. He had started school and was doing very well. In fact, Daniel was doing so well the state hospital had him do a practicum there for three months that summer.

Daniel was seen as a high-functioning person with a mental illness, and because he worked hard and took his medicines responsibly, he was asked to come to some meetings.

Later, Daniel became the Chairperson for the Mental Health Planning Commission. When it came to making decisions about funding for the Mental Heath Centers and the state hospital, he had to throw his weight toward the Mental Health Centers. It was believed they could keep people from going to the state hospital, which people believed was not working. The hospital would get people back in almost the same shape they were in when they left. Daniel became a member of the organization known as the Alliance for the Mentally Ill (AMI). He was soon made a board member. Wyoming AMI made an error, hiring a man as their director who had a history of poor account-ing. He had made an error in the amount of $10,000 in unpaid taxes. The mental health system in the state of Wyoming was changing. The state hospital was the center of focus to be sued.

Daniel's schooling paid off. He passed with excel-lent grades. He improved his writing skills and had a formula for taking multiple question tests. He read everything they threw at him. Daniel could tell some teachers did not think he could make it. He made an extra effort to pass with high grades, and not just to pass. He made it so they could not refuse him. After those two years, Daniel asked Kathy for more. His grades were great. Kathy did not seem surprised by his grades like he thought she would be. He believed he could get him a Bachelor's Degree. The work was harder, but he knew if he could get a Bachelor's Degree, he could get a great job. Daniel had no idea what he was getting into. He was writing, doing practicums, reading and taking tests with a passion. His scores, again, where very high. Daniel completed his Bachelor's Degree in Social Work (BSW) with honors, and he also earned an ASW (Associate Social Work) degree and an Associate of Communications degree. Kathy asked, "What are you going to do now?" Daniel had heard that a Master's Degree was the next step, so he thought it was his next option.

Wyoming schools did not offer a Master's Degree program, so Daniel looked around in other states. He was in Arizona at ASU for a conference and asked them about a Master's program. They referred him to the University of Kansas, to which he wrote an inquiring letter. Amazingly enough they wrote him back, asking him for some information. One of the questions they asked was what he planned to do with his life after he had a Master's Degree in Social Work (MSW), and why he wanted one. Daniel must have said something right because they asked him to meet them at the Department of Social Welfare at the University of Kansas.

When they accepted him and gave him a scholarship, he was obviously overjoyed.

They put Daniel in the Advanced Standing Program, which ran for a year. They had another two year program as well. When Daniel asked the difference between the two programs, they explained that because he focused on social work in all his schooling, the one-year program would suit him. Daniel felt his mother would have been very proud of him. Even though she passed away years ago, he felt she was always there for him. Memories of her empowered him, and he knew Kathy Cassidy believed in him.

A lot of his MSW work was not so much about others but was about himself. The school wanted Daniel to see a psychiatrist, and his first thought was, "What have I done?" When he asked why he needed to do this, he was told every student had to see somebody about their stability. So he went and saw the psychiatrist several times. They would meet in her office, walk, and talk. She told him he would be better off staying away from his sisters due to what she called 'The Queen Bee Syndrome,' which, apparently, is a female hierarchy that only accepts men who are useful to them, while the others who are independent die off.

As Daniel was coming to the end of his schooling, he had one professor who really challenged him.

He dressed like an undertaker and had Daniel writing about death and dying. He told Daniel, the first paper he wrote was worthless. Daniel had never in all his schooling had a paper rejected. The professor had Daniel go to a funeral home to see the equipment they used there, as well as a dead body. At that time Daniel had only seen one other body—his mother's. This was a difficult assignment, to say the least.

At last school was over! This made him nervous because he could not get a C or a lower grade in any class. At the commencements the instructors started gathering the graduates together and putting them in line. It was only then Daniel knew he had passed! He had reached the pinnacle of his life. People cheered for him as he went up on the stage. Some of the professors there encouraged him. The Dean of Social Work congratulated him as she handed Daniel his diploma and shook his hand. He had received the best education anyone could ever ask for, and he did it all while living with and taking medications for his mental illness. As Daniel was leaving the building, the old, grief-stricken professor came up to him and shook his hand with fervor. Daniel realized he was actually teaching him about his own grief process. Daniel understood this process well now, and he could not have asked for a better instructor. All of Daniel's instructors at the University of Kansas were and probably still are the very best. No one can ever take away what they taught him and what he has done with his knowledge.

It took Daniel about five years to complete school. He worked at it as if it were a job. His grade point average was 3.67 overall. Daniel would not give in or give up. He was licensed with the Wyoming State Licensure Board one year after graduating with an MSW. He now held an (LCSW) as a Licensed Clinical Social Worker. He has held his license ever since 1993. After becoming licensed, Daniel has always worked at his craft, except for during one month between jobs. During which time he worked for a pizza parlor. This was hard for him and even harder with his mental-health situation. There are always those who are stigmatized and who lack respect, but if there is no shame there is no stigma, only disgruntled human beings.

MARRIED LIFE

While Daniel was pursuing his education, he married a wonderful woman named Vicky. She had a Bachelor's Degree in Education. Vicky encouraged Daniel to excell in school. She made school easier for him by taking care of the cooking, cleaning, and helping with the bills. The odd thing to Daniel was she had been drawing Social Security and did not work. He also felt it was strange that she did not help him with his school expenses. When Daniel's schooling was over, they went to see his dad and uncle. Then they returned to the school for graduation.

Vicky was anorexic and bulimic, and she decided she did not want help with it, consequently becoming very ill. Daniel had to take her to a mental hospital in Casper. There she found some people from a twelve-step program who advised her to divorce him. Of course Daniel became angry, and he told her if a divorce was what she wanted he would not stop her.

She kept calling and asking him not to let her be taken to the state hospital. It was a traumatic time for both of them.

When there was no other way to change her mind about the divorce, Daniel packed some things and left for Sheridan, Wyoming. Not only were people from the twelve-step program convincing her to leave him, but so was a person who held the same type of degree he had—her counselor. In Sheridan, Daniel found a small apartment to hold up in for a while. He was in the middle of an emotional upheaval. Suicidal thoughts were crossing his mind. Moreover, he was out of money and could not find a job.

Daniel saw a therapist and a doctor who, in the end, sent him to a mental hospital in Casper—the same one his now ex-wife had been in. They did not keep him long and were planning to send him to Yuma, Arizona, where his dad was, which was also where his dad and he had worked in 1973. It seemed like Daniel always ended up in the same old places. Daniel's sister took him to Sheridan from the mental hospital, where he picked up his white Ford pickup truck and belongings. Then he headed to Yuma. "It's better than 'bus therapy,'" he thought. "Catch your breath; you are going to need it after this." Daniel's dad and he talked about him not feeling like working and how he was always better after leaving the state hospital. They decided it would be a good place for Daniel to recover, so Pete took him there.

While he was there, a therapist told him his story and then wanted to hear Daniel's. When he was done, he went ahead and filled the therapist in on the fact he was an alcoholic and he had used some drugs in the past. So instead of treating Daniel like a mental patient, which is how he had always been treated, the therapist treated him like a mental patient with alcohol and drug problems. Once they patched Daniel up, Pete and his wife, Bernice, brought his truck up from Lordsburg, New Mexico. He had left it on some property his dad had there. Daniel's dad was always good to him. After bringing his truck to him and buying him a watch and dinner, they headed back to Lordsburg. Daniel was headed back to Casper the next day.

By now it was winter, while driving back to Casper Daniel ran into a white out. There was a driving wind, snow, and slick roads. For part of the trip, Daniel could not see anything at all in front of him. He was driving blind, praying to God he would not go off the road. Amazingly enough, he did not! The storm cleared up at Rawlins, Wyoming. Daniel called some friends from Casper, Wyoming to see if they could find him a place to stay when he got there. They got him a place that was not fit to live in. Daniel was at the bottom, only way to go was up.

Daniel's friend, Kathy Cassidy, had gone to work at the mental health center. She came and told him he should get some credit cards and find a new place to live, so he did. She also said he should go into a twelve-step program, just as Daniel was advised to do in the state hospital in Evanston. Daniel was still upset with those who had come between his ex-wife and himself. So instead of going to the twelve-step program he needed, he went to the other one. Daniel found out what a mistake he had made when he got drunk three different times with three different people. He felt lost and discouraged. Daniel then met a lady who attempted to show him a different path. He went to a place that was forbidden ground to him. He had to ask those who had disrupted his life for help. This was pure irony of the gravest kind.

Amazingly enough, Daniel found some friends, but his illness was not through with him. Just as things were changing for the better, they got worse. He had started working for a home health care service part time. This, along with his SSDI check, got him by. Daniel once again started losing it mentally. He ended up back in the mental hospital his ex-wife and he had been to before. Daniel's medications failed. He got out with the help of a good doctor. The doctor did not want him to leave just yet, but he did not understand why at the time. The doctor had to switch Daniel's medication again, and since he could not work, he visited the Central Wyoming Counseling Center's drop in. Daniel now as a patient who took part in their drug and alcohol program for those who have dual diagnoses. Daniel realized he should go to the twelve step program he was asked to. This went well at times. He got away from the program for a while and did some wandering. He got totally inhibrihated the last time he drank. It was a Halloween night not easy to forget and hasn't used anything since and is much the better for it.

Later, Daniel started to go back to his friends at the twelve-step program. His closest friend there had developed cancer. He had been working part time for a hospice program—again the excruciating irony of life. It was time for Daniel to make a change. He developed another close relationship. He was put on a new medication requiring blood tests every two weeks. He was also hired part time at the Brain Injury Association. There he found some people could be helped with therapy while others said they could not. This job ended when his supervisor resigned. The old supervisor made it impossible for Daniel to stay by cutting his hours and wages in half..

The medication he was taking was great. Daniel became stronger mentally. He wanted a new start, so he went to Lordsburg, New Mexico, where his dad had passed away and was buried. The new doctor Daniel was seeing, had his nurse handle Daniel's blood work and medications. From there he launched his campaign. Bernice, Daniel's Step mother, drove him to different places, where he dropped off resumes and picked up applications, all to no avail. Daniel waited about one year to hear from someone, during which time he occasionally attended twelve-step meetings. Then he received two job offers on the same day. One was in New Mexico near where he lived and the other was in Northern Wyoming. Daniel chose the job in Wyoming because they called first. He packed some things and left the next day. His employer told him the first client he would see was an alcoholic. After he interviewed this patient, he found the patient was eighteen years old and he had hardly ever had a drink. Daniel was not convinced he was an alcoholic. Therefore, he did not feel comfortable labeling him as one as this would follow him the rest of his life. Needless to say, Daniel was fired.

Daniel went back to New Mexico. He got the doctor instead of the nurse to evaluate him. The doctor changed his medication. A few weeks later, Daniel was

at the Gila Medical Center, where he had some star-
tling revelations.

GILA MEDICAL CENTER

After a doctor changed Daniel's medication, he began preparing for the Licensure exam—a bar exam to become a counselor for New Mexico. On the day of the test, Daniel was filled with extreme anxiety, and he could feel himself starting to decompensate. Decompensatation occurs when part of the brain begins to atrophy and speech is affected as well as other parts of the brain. He called his uncle, who was nearby in Albuquerque, and asked if he could pick him up and take him to the hospital in Albuquerque. The hospital did not keep Daniel. He could only imagine what his uncle thought about his psychotic episode. Later, Daniel's uncle had his son take Daniel to Lordsburg. After a couple of days there, Daniel had another episode, and he had his cousin take him to the Gila Medical Center, where he was admitted to the mental health pod.

The doctors there took him off all of his medication. He became manic, and his paranoid thinking made him ask for Clozzaaril—a psychotropic medication for schizophrenia and reality, the doctor in Wyoming had prescribed this for him earlier. They attempted to give Daniel the same type of medicine the doctor in Silver City had prescribed. It was called Resperidol which failed. It was an anti-psychotic like the clozzaril which did work. .

Daniel said something the doctors didn't like when he did not want to come in from the patio. Five men grabbed him to bring him back in. They felt Daniel's strength and commented on it. He was trying to manipulate them into giving him the Clozzariel. Instead they strapped him to a bed and gave him an injection. A little while later, they let him out of the restraints and gave him the Clozzariel.

MY SMALL, LOST,
LITTLE FRIEND

While Daniel was in the mental health ward, an elderly woman came to stay there. She was small and wrinkled, and no one could understand her. Daniel's doctor had faith in him, and he asked him to see what he could find out about the lady. Daniel used a special tool in cases like this: he offered her a cigarette, which she gladly accepted. Then he asked what her name was, and she told him. At that point Daniel withdrew so as not to overwhelm her. Later, he again approached her, offering her another cigarette and this time asking where she was from. She told him that she was from Chicago but she had gotten lost in California. Daniel asked her how she came to be there but she did not know. After that, each time Daniel approached her with a cigarette he obtained more information about her. He discovered she had been a nurse in the military. She was a darker-skinned

African-American women who was kind and gentle. She called him Mr. Daniel.

Daniel relayed the information he had been told by the little old lady to the front desk. He did not think the front desk believed him, but with the information they obtained from Daniel, they learned both her family and the Federal Bureau of Investigation were looking for her. When it came time for him to leave, Daniel left her all the cigarettes he had and said his good-byes.

SPIRITUAL LINGUISTICS

Daniel was not a hundred percent better yet, but was getting there. He started having certain thought patterns reminding him of something like the Da Vinci Code. For instance, he thought about the twelve nationalities ending with the "ish" suffix, such as: Irish, English, Scottish, Spanish, Turkish, Swedish, and so on. There were also the nationalities ending in "an": American, African, Australian, and so forth. The bible refers to the twelve tribes of Israel and the great multitude, which Daniel understood with more clarity.

Then Daniel's thoughts took off on another track having to do with names. God, he thought, has many names, as do his immediate family members. For instance: God and Gabriel, with Gabriel being female, Michael and Mary, Emanuel and Mary, and Daniel and Destiny. Gabriel has the last three initials "iel," as does Daniel. Michael the archangel's name ends in "ael". Emanuel, who is Jesus, has a name that ends in "uel."

As Adam had three sons, Daniel thought, who were called Cain, Abel, and Seth, and Noah had three sons—Jappath, Ham, and Shem—so too does God: Emmanuel, Michael, and Daniel.

Cain and Jappath are similar in that the word China begins with a C and Japan begins with a J, and the people in both have the mark of Cain in their foreheads, which is the oriental eye. This does not mean they are evil, only they are the children of Cain.

God has paid attention too. As for Abel and Ham, Ham's son Cush was to be the slave of his brothers because of an event that involved Noah. The slaves of the centuries came forth and built Egypt and Africa from one end to the other. Seth a son of Adam, and Shem a son of Noah, whose lineage went to Abraham became two nations. The brown nation, which was to be a great nation, and the nation of Israel. Notice the last three letters in Israel; they are the same as the last three of Michael.

The immediate family of God holds names such as Gemini and Gemini (the twins) who possess the spirit of the lion. The Ancient of Days, I am that I am, Yaway and God are a few of Gods, names. God is my Judge is the meaning of the name Daniel, which is comple-

mented by Justice. There are also Jupiter
Standing on the planet Jupiter, you hav
when you look up, a new heaven.

These thoughts came and went, building themselves up as they continued. Daniel was once told he spoke with many different accents. One therapist even told him he spoke with an Irish or Scottish accent. From what Daniel understood after being told by other people, he frequently spoke with many different accents. Kathy Cassity was one of the people that let him know when he was speaking with foreign accents. Some of the accents he used included French, German, Irish, and even English and Spanish. Daniel did not notice when he was doing this. He began thinking differently. Maybe his thoughts were taking over and he felt he needed to "live in those thoughts." These thoughts and actions were too organized to be coincidental. As they are clearly understood, they may or may not be associated with mental illness but possibly from a mentally ill imagination. A story follows about a dream which seems irrelevant, however it came to Daniel one night, and he pondered over it and wanted to keep it secret. He did so until recently when he felt compelled to reveal the secret he kept, to share with a friend who needed it. It was a man who might lose his family and needed a source of empowerment.

THE DAY OF DOMINION

The creation of the dinosaurs occurred before that of Eden. There was a time lapse between the two creations. At one point the great Pyramid at Giza had spun down on the earth, with a square base sloping at an angle downward and a triangular diamond for its top. The diamond which gave its power to the base and the mighty Sphinx which lay near it came to land on a barren plain. The Pyramid held two members from the heavens which have endured upon the earth.

A closer look at a dollar bill will give its dimensions. The base had a golden cover to it and with its pinnacle made it look like other pyramids surrounding it. It had a diamond top powerful with a spiritual energy of its own as did the spiritual creatures which it brought. Most other pyramids with the same shape and form attempted to rival it but to no avail.

The diamond top after its arrival soon left and began spinning its way up into the heavens after dropping it's base and payload. At the same time, it began creating upon the earth mammoth trees and still and flowing waters as well as wind, rain, dust, and gold dust.

Then came the dinosaurs each of its own kind. Some with sharp talons and teeth, which feasted on the mammoth trees. Over thousands of years they ate the foliage and diminished their source of food and the air they breathed. One by one they fell and the new creation of Eden began.

The Pyramid does not stand alone and its diamond has yet to rest on its base. The Sphinx which lies near the Pyramid, when it was whole before its erosion, was covered in gold as was the base of the Pyramid for space travel. It was told to the ancients, one day the spinning diamond top will return and lock onto its base and bring the necessary rain, wind, and dust and gold dust to renew the Pyramid and Sphinx. There are possibly 3 other Pyramids nearby the Sphinx which will under go the same process. The Sphinx at one time was alive. It was the guardian of the Pyramid and the pair that it brought to earth.

Inside the Pyramid a story is told. In the upper chamber, holding at what looks like a horse trough yet larger and missing a piece in its interior, is a space large enough to fit two people. The missing piece will be replaced on the bed in the upper chamber when the diamond returns. The upper chamber will hold it a new. When the spinning top returns so will the rain, wind and dust and gold dust. Afterwards, they will travel to a new heaven and earth. The earth is most likely Jupiter according to its size, position and name. And once it is stood on, up above will be a new heaven. Its name is a female name another for Gabriel as Jahova is another name for God. The Gemini twins have other names as well, They are Judgment and Justice and they are the ones who ride the Pyramid whose protector is the mighty Sphinx.

CCCC AND CWCC

One day Daniel received a call from a psychiatrist at the Carbon County Counseling Center in Rawlins, Wyoming. They wanted him to come in for an interview; Daniel got the job! He was to be a substance abuse and mental health counselor, as well as a peer supporter. You see, the thing about Daniel is that he wore many hats. He had his own mental health condition. He saw a psychiatrist, Dr. Vuolo, in Casper, Wyoming for his medications. He drove to Casper every two months. Daniel used to work there, only the building had changed. Mike Huston had granted him the privilege to do this. Daniel could never thank him enough. He felt Mike never gave up on him. He worked for CWCC for about a year. It was his first job out of school.

Later in life he worked for The Carbon County Counseling Center in Rawlins, Wyoming. Where Daniel wore many hats to include: substance abuse counselor, mental health counselor, and peer support specialist. He did what was asked of him. He helped start a NAMI chapter in Rawlins, Wyoming. Daniel worked hard at the Carbon County Counseling Center because he felt his work was appreciated. He had good people to work with. Peggy Hayes, his clinical director and later as his Director, gave him assignments and supervised him. Daniel could not have done better under her direction. Daniel could not have asked for more. He liked it when people had confidence in him and utilized his strengths. Who wouldn't?

This book's title is: *The Spirit of the Lion* for a reason. Daniel is a spiritual person, and he backed it up in writing this book. He believes he has experienced much in his life. And is grateful for it.. There would be no children in his life, and he believed this was why God had given him the life he had, his life being filled with the spirit, some times more than at other times, he possess the spirit of the lion. He could never have achieved what he had, helping people with mental illness, their families and other professionals, if it were not for his own illness and the people in his life who had known what had happened. This meant everything to Daniel. He was now freely returning to others what he was freely given..

GETTING WHAT WE DESERVE THROUGH LABORS AND SUCCESS

Do we get what we deserve? The answer is sometimes. Daniel had many different kinds of jobs during his life, with various duties. His first job was selling and delivering his grandmother's potholders door to door. He was paid fifty cents for each one he sold. Daniel found he sold more potholders if he dressed in ragged clothing. He enjoyed looking and acting a little bit poor. This became one in a long series of employment endeavors that continually empowered him.

Later Daniel mowed lawns, shoveled walks, and delivered newspapers. He learned the importance of responsibility by delivering papers in the deep snow and bitter cold—sometimes with the help of his mother, who drove him around.

When he was in high school, Daniel worked week-ends on Casper Mountain. He moved snow, picked up garbage, cut and delimbed trees, bucked and split logs, and blazed trails. He also performed similar work at Alcova Lake. Sometimes he had fun, and other times the crew would kick back in the truck and bullshit with each other.   Daniel did not drink much, but he smoked pot. He took a few hits of LSD in those days, and smoked hash-ish and thystick. Daniel stayed away from speed and downers because he did not like the way he felt when using them. Daniel ceased off of drugs and alcohol after having being reunited to his dad.

After re-connecting with his dad, Daniel spent a year building a gold mine in the Yuma Desert. Daniel's next important job was working for P.A. Incorporated, in Wyoming. It was a pipe inspection company. The crew traveled all over Wyoming and the surrounding states. The people who worked there had a tendency to go to bars after work. They worked long hours in the middle of nowhere, often faced with bitter cold and high winds. Part of Daniel's job was training new people who would eventually go to work for new crews.

Daniel did not know what drove him to work so hard. He had an insatiable appetite for hard work. He was a workaholic. When he left, he did so because a good friend of his had died when he and five other people had a rollover accident in a work transport truck while they were high on pot. For a short while after the accident, he lost his stomach and his heart for work.

Daniel's next job was with the Wyoming Highway Department, where he worked as a dispatcher. He could make the radio hum. In all his jobs, he could pick up the tools of the trade and use them resourcefully. Daniel worked for the Wyoming Highway Department for about one year, quitting after they transferred him to the road crew because he had great difficulty driving their trucks. He even tore the transmission out of one. He also turned to marijuana and alcohol during the last few months that he worked for the Wyoming Highway Department, and a grocery store as well. Daniel lost both jobs when he overdosed on alcohol, weed, and his medication. He abandoned ship.

After that, Daniel was out of work for a while. He found work after, living in a hospital in California where his dad had took him for treatment. When he left, he went to work for the Wyoming Machinery Co. It was a large building and when they moved, it was into a huge building. They were a Caterpillar Company and had enough nuts and bolts that his dad could build three caterpillars out of it. . Daniel started as a parts man and later became the person in charge of the parts return department..

He was forced to resign because his doctor would

not give him the medication he needed because he failed to make an appointment. He was able to work because of the medication. Daniel would not see him due to a lack of awareness of his situation, so the doctor complained to his employer. After he lost his job and was out of medicine Daniel was hospitalized in San Diego by his dad.. Upon his release, he became involved with a good-looking blond whom he had met in the hospital. After working at a water purification plant in Burbank for a while, he had to leave because he could not make enough money. The two of them fled to Wyoming. They split up once they were back in Casper. The next few months were dismal. Daniel worked cleaning two laundry mats, which he hustled, and he drew Social Security Disability. Later on in the spring, Daniel's brothers Dave and Jack went with him to Casper Mountain to cut firewood for money. Daniel used the splitter a lot; he was generally on the mountain from early morning until early in the evening. His brothers mostly performed the deliveries and loaded and unloaded the trucks. Daniel had to help unload the last load. They never paid him much and they always offered him pot, which he took at first when taking down the last load of the day. However, he stopped smoking pot ever since beginning college, until later when he became ill..

In college Daniel started by taking two courses in the fall semester—Sociology and Psychology. He passed both with high grades. He also learned how to study and take tests effectively. Daniel's medication held up. It worked! In the five years he spent going through his undergraduate and graduate programs, he maintained a GPA of 3.67. Daniel read everything they threw at him in his undergraduate program at Casper College and the University of Wyoming. He read most of what he needed to graduate from his Masters program at The University of Kansas. At the university, he was put into the advanced standing program and learned more about himself than ever before. He had to get past a female psychiatrist who gave him some very helpful advice, which he took. It was described as The Queen Bee Syndrome, where one female in a group of them runs what transpires between all the others and the males serve the queen or are gotten rid of. Of course she was talking about his family and other such groups.

Each instructor was looking for qualities in Daniel. They focused on his strengths and challenged him. The instructor for Daniel's class on death and dying put him to the test. He turned back Daniel's paper, which had never happened to him before. Daniel could not get a C, and his instructor acted like he could not make it through his course. Daniel took two classes from him.

The other was a mediation course in which he earned an A. It was the other class that Daniel was unsure about. This instructor was called Stanly Sterling, and he used Daniel's paper to teach him about grief. All in all, Daniel's efforts to succeed paid off. There were many people who said he could not make it. Some he knew from the Alliance of the Mentally Ill, some were friends and family members, and some were even his instructors.

Daniel's, dad and his wife, Bernice supported his going to college. By encouraging him. In his undergraduate work, Daniel once took 22 hours in a semester. And ended up with two C's. Daniel did this to see what his limits were. He found out and backed off from taking more hours than were expected. He also got a C in a problem solving class. In junior high school, Daniel was skilled at math, but not his Algebra. He had to take beginning algebra again in college, and he did well enough to get by.

Somewhere in Daniel's thinking he was more concrete than abstract but he had some of both. College for him became his passion. He loved it more than any other work. It was challenging and achievable. Pete, Bernice, and others were very proud and happy for Daniel. If he were not as old as he became, he would do it again.

Later in life, Daniel's vision deteriorated and his comprehension waned. His ability to read, both out loud and to himself, suffered. However, Daniel never gave up the work he had prepared for. Writing is still one of his strengths; computers have been a great help as well in writing. They made changes easier. As mentioned before, Daniel worked at the Central Wyoming Counseling Center. He worked with those who have had mental illnesses. As he started, one question was asked of him by Wally his youngest professor, he recalled "What will you do if your medication fails and you become ill again?"

"I will get different medications" Daniel replied, "and when I am well again, I will start over." Daniel's father had taught him that no one could take his education or experience away. This was something his dad and he had discussed, and one year later it was proven to be true.

After his medications did fail, Daniel worked for a home health agency and did well for a while. When he became ill and his thinking was incomprehensible, he stopped working for a while. When he went back to work, he felt that his employer lacked trust in him. Daniel quickly sought out another part time job at a hospice. He also found a twelve step program and finally made some friends. When Daniel lost this job because of his illness, he became depressed. He realized that this type of work did not suit him. When he thought back, he realized that Stanly had been right; Daniel had difficulty dealing with grief, death, and dying. This knowledge empowered him to not yet give up his profession.

After wandering alone for a while, feeling lost and lonely, Daniel's doctor found a type of miracle drug for him. The medication was called Clozzaril. He took this along with two other medications—Lithium and Clonazapam. Daniel went through a transfiguration unlike anything he had ever experienced. His thinking was clearer. He was able to think things through. His judgment was good. He could read, write, and help others—both clients and twelve step members.

Daniel's next job was working with a brain injury association. His job was to counsel people and their families. Some people said that counseling could not help these people, but Daniel disagreed. With his enhanced ability to think, he was able to help these people gain understanding where others had lacked the ability to do so. He believed that although these people had brain damage, they still had emotions and thoughts that should not be ignored and could not be denied. Daniel also believed that they, like other people, might have mental and emotional issues that needed to be addressed. It seemed that others thought that it was easier to effectively store them in warehouses. There are, of course, those for whom medical support is necessary.

Daniel's supervisor was leaving her job, and this made it impossible for him to stay. She cut his time and wages in half, so he felt he had to resign. Daniel took a sabbatical to New Mexico where his dad had lived. Bernice and Dave were there too. While living in Lordsburg, New Mexico, Daniel continued to take his wonderful new medications and hunted high and low for a job. Bernice drove him to different cities to further his search. Daniel did not know how she knew where to go. His dad was like that too when it came to finding his way around any community large or small. They both possessed the uncanny ability to do so. They knew north, south, east, west and no town no matter how large or small was a stranger to them.

Finally, Dave and Bernice were gone, they moved away from Lordsburg. And shortly after they left there was good news. Suddenly, Daniel was offered two jobs in the same day. One was in Powell, Wyoming, and the other was in Las Cruces, New Mexico. The first job offer was for a position as a therapist, and the second for a position as a substance abuse counselor. Daniel felt that God was with him that day. He chose the job in

Powell, Wyoming. When he drove up there, he could not find decent housing.

Daniel was let go from his position as a therapist because he refused to label an eighteen year old an alcoholic. He returned to Lordsburg, but the position in Las Cruces had already been filled. Upon his return, his doctor in Silver City took him off one of the miracle drugs. Daniel felt the reason his doctor did this was he did not want to keep up with the periodic blood tests that were required of people who take Lithium, and also Clozzaril because Daniel had not taken the job he had been offered.

Daniel's condition again began to deteriorate, and he was hospitalized once more, in the Gila Medical Center. He explained to the hospital that his medications had been switched. After being briefly put in four-point restraints, the staff decided that their medications were not working for Daniel, so they put Daniel back on Clozzaril.

The prescribing doctor in Silver City one of two who cut Daniel off his meds, set up a court hearing. The object of this hearing was to permanently send Daniel to a New Mexico state institution. When the doctor testified, Daniel accused him of being a liar. Many other people including his brother and other members of his family, as well as a mental-health support team bore weight on the court . Eventually, Daniel got the chance to tell his side of the story. He told the truth that the doctor did not follow his Dr. in Wyoming's instructions.

The judge ordered the hospital to put Daniel back on his original medication to stabilize him, allowing the hospital thirty days to do so. After thirty days had passed, Daniel was ready to go. He had found a job with the help of Kathy Cassidy in Casper Wyoming. Daniel also received help from the Baptist church that he had begun attending with Bernice. Members of the Baptist church took him from the hospital. Daniel had some money, and he rented a U-Haul truck. Then he spent the night at the preacher's house. After the truck was loaded with his car hitched behind it, Daniel paid a driver to take him non-stop to Rawlins, Wyoming—a small prison town. Daniel's new job was in Wyoming, at the Rawlins Thrift Store. He worked there for about eight months, during which time he met some interesting people. He helped them with the State Department of Developmental Disabilities.

Daniel's next job was with the Department of Vocational Rehabilitation. One week prior to becoming a permanent employee for the state, he resigned because his supervisor wanted him to. Daniel believes that she wanted an all-female team and that she wanted his resignation to appear to be his own decision. Daniel spent the next six months working for himself in a private practice. He also took a job delivering pizzas. This was the only menial job he had had since he had become licensed to work as a social worker. One day, out of the blue, Daniel got a call from a psychiatrist to interview for a position with the Carbon County Counseling Center. They hired him! He has been there ever since. His work involves substance-abuse and mental-health counseling, as well as peer support. He likes his job and co-workers. Remember that Daniel said that God was with him that day? He gave Daniel the mental-health and substance-abuse therapist position in a place he would have never expected to be. Daniel got what he felt he deserved. A poem about differences and sameness in life among all Gods creatures,and an editorial about the greatest foe for those that have had a mental health situations follows.

ANIMAL CRACKERS

This Poem came to Daniel when he came to the ending of his writing this book, It has several deep meanings and should be read with a rhythm

Unlike animal crackers, all animals have different colors and codes. Take, for instance, the Saint Bernard—a white and reddish-brown creature. Like a Clydesdale horse is larger than other horses, the Saint Bernard is larger than most other dogs. The Bald Eagle fits this description as well. The White Stallion and the Chalet cow, along with doves are all white. Take cows, for instance. They are black, black and white, or white and brown, and there are also Hereford bulls whose coloring is similar to the coloring of the Saint Bernard. We have all seen Black Horses and horses with different color schemes. In different countries, we find animals with other, exotic color schemes. We easily identify lions, tigers, cats, panthers, and mountain lions as belonging to the same group.

Each animal has its own strengths, weaknesses, and color schemes due to its unique genetic code. If you could track back your own genetic code, how far back would it go? Would it go back to the beginning of man, or be a branch of it? Where have we come from and where will we go. Would you have to have a certain color code like the animals, birds, and fishes of the sea? Are we not more like the creatures we share the world with than we know? Think of all the antlered animals and ask yourself, "How are they like me?" The Crow, Black Angus, and black stallion are solid in color. Which color came first: white, black, brown, or red? Or was there only one color to begin with, or two? So much for the animal crackers. So much for an expanding universe.

WHEN WILL
DISCRIMINATION END

Discrimination can be defined as a lack of respect or injustice against race, creed, color, religion, employment or disability. It can be hateful, abusive, relentless, traumatizing and self-seeking, and it effects both those who are discriminated against and those who discriminate. Advocacy programs have been developed for those who are unable to protect or defend themselves.

Discrimination can be observed in certain types of employment, income levels, housing circumstances, and certain physical illnesses. While many have heard about racial and religious discrimination, not so many have heard of discrimination on the basis of a mental-health disability.

Who would discriminate against a person with physical disabilities? Not many, you might think, but discrimination against the mentally ill happens all the time. For instance, in some communities a small number of people work to push housing programs for the mentally ill to the outskirts of towns and cities. They also seek to move them to another community. Why? I believe that they do it to protect themselves from something they fear and do not understand.

If a person could catch mental illness like a cold, we'd all have it. Leprosy was thought to be contagious a few hundred years ago; however, modern science has proven that this is not the case. Mental illnesses are caused by brain disorders, which are observable physical changes in the brain. They are not contagious.

Others discriminate against the mentally ill because they believe that they are more likely to commit crime. In fact, there are fewer reported cases of crimes being committed by persons with mental illness per capita than among the general population of the U.S. When the mentally ill do commit crime, it is often more highly publicized, which makes it appear to be more common.

Most people with mental illness are unable to engage in what is considered criminal thinking; they are unable to be cold and calculating, and their illness generally causes them to isolate themselves and withdrawal from society, rather than acting aggressive. A person does not acquire a mental illness because they are a bad person, and they can still achieve good things with the proper support. Once a mental illness is discovered, the afflicted person can function normally when they are given medication and assistance, and encouraged not to withdraw from others, but are encouraged to work and play, and learn about their illness among other things.

We have made great strides in this country against discrimination. For the first time in our country's history, the people in the United States have elected a black president. Do we still have racial discrimination? Yes, even though the white population will become the minority in the next ten years, due to the growth of the Hispanic subpopulation.

This may have a dramatic and positive impact on our culture, and will possibly affect our propensity for discrimination. Hopefully, we can continue to put aside our racial differences.

It is time to also begin accepting the mentally ill as legitimate contributing citizens as well. We all have much more to gain by embracing the many differences we have rather than discriminating against each other. And this is only the beginning.

Daniel Meyers LCSW/Peer Support Specialist

LaVergne, TN USA
31 October 2010
202946LV00001B/33/P